WHY WOULD A GOOD GOD ...?

WHY WOULD A GOOD GOD ...?

*Finding Peace with Evil,
Death, and Pain*

PATTI GORDON

&Deepwater Press
Atlanta, Georgia

WHY WOULD A GOOD GOD …?
Published by Deepwater Press

Copyright © 2021 by Patricia Gordon
International Standard Book Number: 978-1-940084-08-4

Cover photo by Rudy Issa on Unsplash

Unless otherwise indicated, Scripture quotations are from:
New American Standard Bible
©1960, 1971, 1977, 1995 by The Lockman Foundation
Other Scripture quotations are from:
Holy Bible, New International Version (NIV)
©1984, International Bible Society
Holy Bible, New Living Translation (NLT)
©1996, Tyndale House Publisher, Inc.
All rights reserved.

ALL RIGHTS RESERVED
All rights reserved. No part of this book may be
reproduced or transmitted in any form or by any means
without written permission from the author.

For information:
DEEPWATER PRESS
880 Marietta Hwy · Suite 630-170 · Atlanta, GA 30075

*To Margie, Kathy, Barbara, Janet, and Karen:
precious sisters, lifelong friends, and patient
teachers of all that matters in the end.*

Contents

Chapter 1: The Question 9
Chapter 2: Why Does God Allow Evil? 14
Chapter 3: Why Does God Allow Death? 24
Chapter 4: Why Does God Allow Pain? 36
Chapter 5: The Beautiful Part 39
Chapter 6: Perfume in the Gas Tank 42
Chapter 7: Don't Make Me 52
Chapter 8: Another Kind of Pain 59
Chapter 9: The Plan 64
Chapter 10: Beyond Pain 70
Chapter 11: The Million 77

Chapter 1

The Question

It doesn't take long to learn this world is not a perfect place.

I've never had a baby, but I've talked to a lot of friends who have. What's more, I've seen a few television shows and, from what I can tell, it takes about three seconds from the time we make our grand entrance till the moment we get our first swat.

So much for paradise.

What's more, the older we get, the easier it is to see that paradise just isn't in this picture.

I grew up hearing about Adam and Eve—how they started out in a beautiful garden walking around with God (yep, *the* God). Then that nasty serpent came along, and things just went to pieces.

Most of my life I wondered why in the world God let that serpent into the garden in the first place. Why did He let him mess up a perfectly perfect world?

The Question

I was in grade school when I realized I wasn't the only one asking that question. I went to a parochial school and, every once in a while, the priest would visit our classroom and we'd get to ask him all kinds of things.

He was such a nice man. We loved the way he smiled when he talked to us and the way he listened so carefully to our questions. Plus, he usually came up with some pretty good answers.

Then one day I decided it was time to ask the Big One. The question that had been bothering me for as long as I could remember.

I raised my hand and waited patiently until he called my name. Then I inquired, "Why does God let bad things happen?" Several of the other kids in class let out a "Yah! Why?!"

The priest paused for a moment then took a deep breath and started speaking in a language I did not understand. Oh, I knew a few words here and there, but most of them had way too many syllables and sounded awfully strange to me. When he finished, I wondered if even he understood what he said.

Decades later, I was still struggling with that same question. By then, I had heard all kinds of answers from pastors, teachers, and people on TV. But somehow, their answers always left me hanging. I'm sure they made perfect sense to a lot of other people. But to me, it seemed like everything they said just danced around the question.

So I kept asking, "If God is good, and if He really has the power to do anything, why does He allow such horrible things to happen?" In my simple brain, the goodness of God and those horrible things just did not go together.

Passing the Ball

Years later, I was still wrestling with that same confounded question. What's more, the phrase, "If God is good …" was beginning to chip away at my belief that God really is good. Worse yet, as my belief in God's goodness began to fade, so did my willingness to trust Him.

It was plain to see the struggle was taking a toll on my faith. I had to find a way to close the book on this one.

So I called out to the only One I knew who surely had the answer. "God, the Bible says You are good, so I promise I *will* believe it. But when I look around at the world You created, I see a lot of bad things." I continued, "I know You are good, and I know bad things happen. Could You please show me how those two things go together?"

I had run out of options. The ball was in His court now. All I could do was wait and hope that, somehow, He would answer.

The Question

A Turtle With Arthritis

When I prayed that prayer, I had no idea whether God would ever see fit to give me an answer—an answer so simple that *even I* could understand it—an answer that would finally give me peace.

Now I clearly see, not only did He answer but His response was immediate. Oh, He did not tell me everything at once. His answer did not come like a bolt of lightning. It came more like a turtle with arthritis.

Little by little, I began to experience a series of events. At the same time, truths from my daily Bible reading began to strike new chords. Together, those experiences and the truths I was learning blended to reveal answers that finally put my heart and mind to rest.

When all was said and done, God answered three questions:

- Why does He allow evil?
- Why does He allow death?
- Why does He allow pain?

What's more, I saw how His goodness and love for us shine in the midst of it all.

Answers

If you've ever asked those same questions or wondered about God's goodness, I'd like to share His answers with you.

Oh, I realize the answers God gave me are not the only ones that exist. People much smarter than me have figured out answers I may never understand. What's more, no doubt God has plenty of answers that are far beyond our human comprehension. After all, He tells us, "My thoughts are not your thoughts, nor are your ways My ways" (Isaiah 55:8).

Yet even though our brains are finite, and we cannot completely understand an infinite God, He gives us the truths of Scripture and His Holy Spirit to guide and teach. He might not reveal all the answers we want, but He will reveal all the answers we need to see through Satan's lies and experience God's perfect peace.

I also realize the answers in this book may not give you the same perfect peace they gave me. At the very least, I pray they will give you a glimpse of God's goodness, sovereignty, and love.

And so I invite you to join me as I do my best to share with you what God has shared with me.

Chapter 2

Why Does God Allow Evil?

During my search for answers about evil, death, and pain, it didn't take long to realize one question was foundational. Without a clear answer to that one, I would never find satisfying answers to the others. That question was: "Why does God allow evil?"

It didn't surprise me when God answered that question first. When He did, He started at the beginning—in this case, the *very* beginning.

The Beginning

It all started one morning when I opened my Bible to the book of Genesis. In chapter one I read about God creating the heavens and the earth—from when He created light to when He created Adam and Eve. The last verse in that chapter says: "God saw all that He had made, and behold, it was very good" (Genesis 1:31).

In chapter two God has a little chat with Adam about the Garden of Eden. God told Adam, "From any tree of the garden you may eat freely; but from the tree of the knowledge of good and evil you shall not eat, for in the day that you eat from it you will surely die" (Genesis 2:16-17).

I have to admit, I scratched my head when I read those verses. Why would God create a tree with fruit He didn't want Adam to eat? He let Adam eat from all the other trees. Why did He put the kibosh on that one?

What's more, why would He parade Adam in front of it and say, "See the fruit on all those trees? That's yours for the taking. But see the beautiful fruit on this one? That's off limits to you!"

I don't know how that strikes you, but it seemed pretty strange to me.

So why did God do it?

I was stumped.

Meet Boo

It wasn't long after my run-in with the second chapter of Genesis that God introduced the next part of His lesson. That part knocked on my front door.

My sweet neighbor and her two little children had been hiking in the woods and ran across a baby blue jay sitting quietly in the middle of the path. The little guy wasn't old enough to fly.

I realize blue jays don't usually tug at our heartstrings. They tend to be pretty obnoxious birds. But this little fellow was cute as a button, and his tiny, round eyes were looking straight up at them.

What's more, just a few feet away, a snake had appeared to be getting ready for a snack. That's when my big-hearted neighbors swooped down, rescued the baby bird, and brought him home, safe and sound.

There was only one hitch. My neighbors were scheduled to move to Florida in two weeks. They couldn't take their little friend with them, so they knocked on my door and asked if I would adopt him.

That baby bird was the cutest ball of gray fluff I'd ever seen. One look at that helpless creature and, of course, my answer was, "Yes!" I welcomed him into his new home and named him Boo—short for Boo Jay.

I didn't have a birdcage. But since Boo was too young to fly, I didn't need one right away. I took a basket, added a branch, and it became Boo's home sweet home.

Boo was perfectly content to sit in his basket or on my finger as I wandered through the neighborhood. He became quite a hit with the neighbors as they stopped to marvel at my sweet, fluffy friend.

Boo sat on my lap when I rocked on the porch or nestled on my stomach when I lay down to watch a movie. Boo became my constant companion.

I worked from home, and Boo loved to help. He perched on my keyboard and watched the cursor crawl across the screen.

Before long, Boo sprouted feathers and began to fly. But he never ventured far from me. Most often, he'd flutter up and sit on my shoulder or fly up and sit on my head.

I fell in love with my loyal little buddy.

Then one day, I was surfing the Web to find out more about raising birds when I ran across something that made my heart sink. The article said it was illegal to own a wild bird or keep one in captivity.

I cried.

I couldn't stand the thought of giving up sweet Boo. But the article was clear—I didn't have a choice. After I dried my tears, I picked up the phone and spent hours searching for a bird rehabilitator who would take Boo in and teach him how to live in the wild, once again.

Even though Boo was mine for only a few weeks, giving him up broke my heart. I had no way of knowing whether he would ever adjust to living outdoors. Or, if he did, how long he would survive in the cold, cruel world. My little feathered friend had captured my heart and it ached for weeks after he was gone.

As time crawled by, I wondered why I was still feeling so sad about losing Boo. I was particularly confused when I remembered a parakeet my family had when I was in grade school.

Dad brought that parakeet home one evening as a surprise for his six little girls. Of course we went wild with excitement.

For almost two years my five sisters and I fed him every day, changed the newspaper in the bottom of his cage, and tried to get him to sit on our fingers. Then one morning we woke up and found him lying on the floor of his cage. It didn't take us long to realize we would never hear his little chirps again.

We had a funeral in the back yard and shed a few tears—but in a couple of days we all felt fine, and life was back to normal.

So why did I grieve so hard when I lost Boo but not so much when we lost our parakeet? That colorful parakeet was much prettier than Boo. Plus, he was ours for a whole lot longer. And wouldn't a little schoolgirl grieve harder and longer over losing a pet bird than a grown woman would?

But there I was, weeks later, with my aching heart still missing Boo. It didn't make sense until, one day, something dawned on me.

Our parakeet didn't have a choice as to where he lived or with whom. Plus, it wasn't hard to guess why he rarely sat on our fingers. He probably didn't consider us very good friends since we kept him in a cage night and day. The poor little guy was stuck with us. He had no choice but to stay.

On the other hand, Boo could go anywhere he wanted. He never spent a single minute in a cage. In fact, he and I spent a lot of time outdoors where he never left my finger. Boo had the freedom to fly away any time he chose. But instead, he chose to stay with me.

Sure enough! That was the clincher. Boo had a choice. He could leave me or not—love me or not—and my sweet Boo chose to stay and love me.

That was what made my relationship with Boo so meaningful and so delightful. Boo chose me, and that was why I, in turn, fell in love with him.

Suddenly, I understood why God would create that tree.

Meet Mr. Algebra

Let me explain it another way. How about a quick trip back to high school?

Ladies, let's say you have a crush on a boy in algebra class. You've admired him from afar for a very long time. You've never said a word to him because you think he's out of your league. In fact, your best friend is the only person you ever told about your dreamboat.

Then one evening your doorbell rings. You open the door and there is Mr. Algebra standing in front of you with a huge bouquet of roses. He asks, "May I have the pleasure of taking you to dinner?"

Sounds like a movie, huh?

After you pick your chin up off the floor, you notice he keeps glancing to the side. You poke your head out the door and take a gander.

What do you know! There's your best friend, a few feet away, pointing a gun at his head and whispering, "Now tell her you love her!"

Wow! Some kind of movie! More like a horror flick!

What would your reaction be? (Other than making a beeline to find a new best friend!)

Ladies, how much would those roses, that dinner invitation, and that proclamation of love mean to you? Or guys, if you were on the doorstep with a gun to your head, how much would that love mean to you?

Or would it even be love?

Of course not! Because love requires a choice. In order for love to exist, there has to be an option not to love.

BACK TO THE TREE

So, let's go back to Genesis chapter two. Why did God create that tree?

I don't know all the theological reasons. But one thing I do know—the moment God created that tree, He gave us an option not to love.

You see, up to that point, everything in paradise was ours for the taking. Nothing was off limits. There were no rules to obey. But when God created that tree and told Adam not to eat its fruit, suddenly we had a choice to obey God's command—or not. And guess what God says about obedience.

In John 14:15, Jesus tells us, "If you love Me, you will keep My commandments." What's more, in 1 John 5:3, the Apostle John tells us, "For this is the love of God, that we keep His commandments."

But why would God equate love for Him with keeping His commandments? The answer is simple: when we love someone, we naturally want to please them. In God's case, we please Him by keeping His commands.

So God created the tree, and His command not to eat from it was His invitation to a meaningful love relationship with Him. That's why, from the very beginning, God always had at least one command on the table. And our response to His command is our answer to His question, "Do you love me?"

The Flip Side of Love

So love is born from choice. And every day God gives us a brand-new set of choices.

Yet as wonderful as each choice to love might be, we cannot forget that each has a flip side. Every choice to love comes complete with a choice *not* to love. The sad part is, when we choose not to love, we eventually end up with evil.

It starts with evil things in our heart—things like selfishness, jealousy, anger, and hate. Then, as we live with those things in our heart, we give birth to more and more evil.

When God gives us the freedom to choose, He takes a risk that we will choose evil. But why would He take that risk? Why does He think the risk is worth it?

The Reason for the Risk

Again, I don't know all the reasons God chooses to take that risk, but one reason is clear: if we don't have the freedom to choose evil, we don't have the freedom to choose love.

Without that choice, we could never experience all the blessings love can bring. We could never love and glorify God by our faith and obedience to Him. What's more, without the freedom to choose, we would be nothing more than robots—and nobody wins with that.

THE BOTTOM LINE

Why does God allow evil? The answer God gave me boils down to two things: *because He loves us*, and *so we, too, can love*.

After years of searching, I was amazed at the simplicity of that answer. I was even more amazed at how His answer could bring such peace to my heart. But my amazement did not end there.

Through it all, God taught me so much more than an answer to my question. Not only did I learn that He is good even though He allows evil, I learned God's goodness is *why* He allows evil.

Now that's a lesson only God could teach.

Chapter 3

Why Does God Allow Death?

When I was 15, my father and two sisters were killed in an automobile accident. Dad was my hero. My sisters were my friends. For years after the accident, I fought fears of abandonment and the pain of losing the father and sisters I loved.

So why would a good God allow death when it leaves such a trail of grief behind? In answering that question, once again God took me back to the beginning.

The Beginning (Again)

When God gave Adam the first command, He clearly warned him of the consequence of disobeying it. Genesis 2:16-17 tells us: "The Lord God commanded the man, saying, 'From any tree of the garden you may eat freely; but from the tree of the knowledge of good and evil you shall not eat, for in the day that you eat from it *you will surely die*'" (emphasis added). Paul repeats that message in Romans 6:23: "The wages of sin is death."

Okay, so we were warned. But that doesn't answer the question. God could have done anything in response to our disobedience. Why did He choose death?

THE SPIRITUAL DEATH STORY

The Bible teaches that Adam and Eve's disobedience resulted in two kinds of death: physical and spiritual.

Before I started reading the Bible I had no idea what spiritual death was. In fact, I'd never even heard of it. But come to find out, it's one of the most important things we can deal with in this life. That's because it matters long after our life on earth is over. In fact, it matters for eternity.

What is spiritual death? Simply put, it is separation from God. And why does spiritual death matter for eternity? The Bible says there are only two places we can go after we die: heaven or hell. God is in heaven. But if we're separated from God … well, you get the picture.

So why did God separate from us after we disobeyed Him? The short answer is because He had to.

Here's why:

- When we disobey God (what the Bible calls sin) we are no longer perfect.

- Because God is perfect, He cannot accept imperfection. What's more, if we are imperfect, God cannot let us into His perfect heaven. In plain language, that means we're headed for hell.
- The real bummer is that every one of us has sinned—even if we've only told one lie in our whole life or stolen one crayon in kindergarten. So, like it or not, after we sin, we're stuck with a one-way ticket to hell. It's as simple as that.
- The worst part is, we can't make ourselves perfect again. That means we cannot reconnect with God on our own. Sin is like a teaspoon of sewage in a pitcher of water. No matter how much sugar we add, it will never make the water pure. No matter how many good things we do, we can never erase the sins we have committed.
- Since we cannot make ourselves perfect again, we're up a creek without a paddle. We cannot reconnect with a perfect God and spend eternity in heaven with Him.
- So there we are—spiritually dead—separated from the God who created us. And the only light at the end of the tunnel is hell. (Not a good thing.)

The Good Thing

Okay, so that's a pretty bleak picture. But the good thing is, this is not the end of the story. Because of His love for us, God went to great lengths (and paid a gargantuan price) to give us a way to reconnect with Him.

Here's how He did it:

- God said He would allow a perfect sacrifice to pay the penalty for our sins. (Sort of like paying a fine to let a criminal go free.)
- But how could we come up with a perfect sacrifice? Nothing on this earth is perfect. (We all made sure of that.)
- That's when our merciful God stepped in and came to our rescue. God gave His only Son, Jesus, to be our perfect sacrifice.
- Jesus took the form of a man, lived a perfect life, then willingly died on a cross to save us.
- He paid the penalty for our sins so God could forgive us and view us as pure and spotless.
- When God sees us as pure and spotless, He can welcome us back into a relationship with Him.
- Then we become—you guessed it—spiritually alive again!

- Because we are spiritually alive (no longer separated from God), we can have a personal relationship with Him that begins here on earth and lasts forever. (Yep! That includes heaven!)

The Choice

So that's the Cliffs Notes version of the spiritual life and death story. But there's something we must not forget: God always gives us a choice. (Remember—no robots.)

We were not born with the gift of salvation, and we certainly don't inherit it. What's more, God doesn't force us to accept it. That leaves only one option.

The only way to receive the gift of salvation is to personally choose to accept it. John 1:12 tells us "To all who believed [Jesus] and accepted him, he gave the right to become children of God" (NLT).

So how do we accept Jesus and, with that, God's gift of salvation? We do it by making a conscious choice to turn from our sin and commit our lives to Him. Jesus put it simply when He said, "Follow Me."

An Important Note

It's important to note that some folks think they can say a quick prayer, tell Jesus they accept Him, then go out and live like the devil.

But God is not fooled. It's not our words that get us into heaven. Yes, God hears our words, but He listens to our heart. He wants to know our heart is sincere and our faith in Jesus is real.

The Acid Test

How can we tell if our faith is real? The acid test is the way we live our lives.

Jesus said, "You will know them by their fruits" (Matthew 7:20). Jesus also said, "By this all people will know that you are My disciples: if you have love for one another" (John 13:35).

In other words, if our faith is real, love and good works will naturally follow. Of course, that doesn't mean we will be perfect. But it does mean we will grow in obedience to Him.

After all, if we *really* understand that we're a hopeless case without Jesus (a.k.a. destined for an eternity of torture in you-know-where), and if we *really* understand how much pain He went through to save us, we will love Him—and I mean *really* love Him.

Remember, when we love someone, we want to make them happy. So good works are the acid test that our faith in Jesus is real. And they are the honest-to-goodness proof that our heart is truly His.

The Way

One more thing before we move on. Jesus said, "I am the way, and the truth, and the life; *no one comes to the Father but through Me*" (John 14:6, emphasis added). The Bible is clear. Accepting Jesus as our Savior and the Lord of our lives is the only way to become a child of God.

Now you might be thinking it isn't fair that God gives only one way back to Him. But remember—God didn't need to take us back. We were the ones who rejected Him. The amazing part is, He *did* give us a way back! What's more, He paid a huge price to make it happen!

So that's the happy ending to the spiritual death story and more proof that God truly *is* a good God who loves us. But we're still not done with the question. What about physical death? What's the story with that?

The Physical Death Story

Why do the wages of sin have to be physical death, too? Did God just get mad and condemn us to the most horrific thing He could think of? The answer to that question, again, goes back to the beginning.

God's original plan did not include physical death. Genesis tells us there was another tree in the garden from which Adam and Eve were free to eat—the tree of life. The Bible says those who ate from the tree of life would physically live forever.

After Adam and Eve sinned, God promised to send a savior—His only son, Jesus. But God also did something else. He blocked us from the tree of life.

Genesis 3:22-24 tells us: "Then the Lord God said, 'Look, the human beings have become like us, knowing both good and evil. What if they reach out, take fruit from the tree of life, and eat it? Then they will live forever!' So the Lord God banished them from the Garden of Eden, and … stationed mighty cherubim to the east of the Garden of Eden. And he placed a flaming sword that flashed back and forth to guard the way to the tree of life" (NLT).

So as soon as sin entered the world, God took the tree of life out of the picture. Without that tree to keep us alive, our bodies were destined to die.

But *why* physical death? I still didn't have an answer.

THE TRIPLE SHOCK

Fast forward a few years to a time when, again, death made a visit way too close to home. I was in my mid-30s when my dear friend, Nancy Quattlebaum, suddenly died. She was healthy one minute—dead on the floor the next. An autopsy revealed a congenital heart defect that no one knew about before it took its final bow.

A couple years later, another dear friend, Mark Hopkins, joined Nancy after a courageous fight with brain cancer. Soon after that, my friend, Matt Tiffany, joined Mark and Nancy when he was hit by a semi on the interstate highway during Christmas vacation.

All in their 30s. All too young. All too precious. All too confusing.

Somehow, that triple shock was the straw that broke the camel's back. Why would a good God take my gifted and godly young friends? Their deaths also reignited my confusion about why God would take my 41-year-old father and my sisters when they were only 10 and 11. They all loved God. They all loved people. They were all making this world a better place.

It was just too cruel.

But God had an answer and, once again, He graciously showed it to me. A week or so after Matt died, I came across a Bible verse that stopped me in my tracks: "Precious in the sight of the Lord is the death of His godly ones" (Psalm 116:15).

Hmm. That one took me back a notch. It had never occurred to me to look at death from God's point of view.

Soon after, I ran across another Bible verse—Ecclesiastes 7:1: "... the day of one's death is better than the day of one's birth." Then another: "We are confident, yes, well pleased rather to be *absent from the body and to be present with the Lord*" (2 Corinthians 5:8, NKJ, emphasis added).

There it was—in three little verses—the answer to my question. Death was not the tragedy I had believed it to be. When I could finally see it from a bigger (and biblical) perspective, I could see that death was actually a blessing.

God cut us off from the tree of life because, if He had allowed us to eat from it, our bodies would live forever. If our bodies lived forever, we would be locked forever in a world filled with evil and pain.

The good news is, if we accept Jesus' gift of salvation, the day of our death *is* better than the day of our birth. That's because on the day we were born, we entered a broken world. But on the day of our death, we enter paradise—a perfect heaven filled with perfect love. Quite a promotion—and a gracious one at that, from a merciful and loving heavenly Father.

THE DOOR

So that was the answer God gave me—the answer that finally gave me peace. Oh, I still feel the pain of losing loved ones, but the pain is not for them. It is only for the few short years I will be on this earth without them. If they, too, have accepted God's gift of salvation, I know I will see them again.

For there will surely come a day when God will open death's door for me. On that day I will walk through heaven's gates and once again run to the arms of my loved ones. What's more, on that day I will finally see Jesus and thank Him, with all my heart, for dying on a cross for me.

The best part is I will never say have to say goodbye, again. We'll be living forever in a perfect paradise filled with beauty, love, and peace.

So why does God allow death? It's because He loves us, and He really *does* want us to live happily ever after.

ONE MORE THING ...

I could not end a chapter about death without addressing one more thing. If you are anything like me, you might be wondering, "If heaven is such a perfect place, why should I stick around here?"

Well, the Bible talks about that, too.

The Bible teaches that God created each of us to fulfill a unique plan and purpose. Psalm 139 tells us that while we were still in our mother's womb, God wrote out His plan for all our days. Verse 16 says, "In Your book were written all the days that were ordained for me, when as yet there was not one of them."

Jeremiah 29:11 even tells us, "'For I know the plans that I have for you,' declares the Lord, 'plans for prosperity and not for disaster, to give you a future and a hope.'"

Yes, God has a plan for you and me, and His plan for us is good.

Oh, I understand that life on earth doesn't always look or feel so good. There have been times I have longed for this life to be over. I know what it's like to search high and low for a single ray of hope. Life can be incredibly painful. What's more, it can feel like the pain will never end.

So the question remains: why should we suffer through the pain of this broken world simply to live out the years God has ordained for us and to fulfill His purpose for our lives?

Hold that thought ... and keep reading!

Chapter 4

Why Does God Allow Pain?

When we were born into a broken world, unfortunately, pain was part of the package. And it has become, to most of us, a very familiar part.

We've all experienced pain. There is no getting around it. It can range from simple annoyance to devastating agony that makes us want to die. Pain can be physical, mental, emotional—a plague for a lifetime or a flash in the pan. But no matter what kind of pain we've experienced, we've all experienced it all too often.

Now comes the $64,000 question. If God really loves us, why does He allow it?

Once again, the answer starts with Adam and Eve.

Back to the Garden

Adam and Eve destroyed our paradise by turning from the only One who could sustain it. With their first foolish choice, they opened the door and ushered in a world of evil.

No more carefree, sinless days. No more flawless relationships. No more impeccable health and prosperity. No more perfect weather. No more gardens without weeds. No more lions and bears that don't bite. All gone with a choice to reject the God who created it all and gave it to His children.

Unfortunately, the rebellion did not end there. Adam and Eve did not make the last foolish choice. After they went off the deep end, everyone else followed suit. That's *everyone*—including you and me.

Yes. We've all chosen evil. We've all come up with a warped idea about what will make us happy. Some people want power and control. Others just want to satisfy their desires any way they choose. Unfortunately, those ideas can lead down some pretty twisted paths, and a lot of people can end up in some awfully miserable places.

So here we are—living in a world filled with the consequences of all our decisions.

Why God allows Pain

When we talk about why God allows pain, it's important to remember that God did not choose pain for us. God chose paradise for His children. We are the ones who chose evil and pain.

Yet even when God sees us make our foolish and rebellious choices, He refuses to take our free will away. (Remember—He's not into robots.) Instead, God allows evil and pain because *He loves us enough to allow us to choose it.*

So that was His answer—at least the bottom line. And, once again, His love for us shines through. But there's more to that answer—so much more. And it's the beautiful part.

Chapter 5

The Beautiful Part

You might be wondering what in the world could be beautiful about pain?

The beautiful part is God's response.

In order to fully appreciate His response, we need to take a look at how the whole thing unfolded from God's point of view.

Turning the Tables

Put yourself in God's place. You created human beings and love them as your children. Because you love them, you gave them a magnificent paradise to call home. You also gave them a choice—the choice to love you or not—the choice to choose good or evil.

They chose to not love you, destroyed their paradise, and filled their world with evil, pain, and suffering. What's more, an awful lot of them blame you for the consequences of the evil things they do.

Now, if you were God, how would you respond? If you're anything like me, it would not be pretty.

So how *does* God respond?

A LOOK AT JESUS

The Bible tells us Jesus is God and "the exact representation of [God's] nature" (Hebrews 1:3). This means that when we see how Jesus responds, we see how God responds.

The Gospel of John tells us, after Lazarus died, Jesus saw Lazarus' friends and sister weeping. When He saw them, it says "[Jesus] was deeply moved in spirit and was troubled" (John 11:33). What's more, John tells us "Jesus wept" (John 11:35).

In Matthew 9:36 we learn, "When [Jesus] saw the crowds, he had compassion on them because they were confused and helpless, like sheep without a shepherd" (NLT).

In Matthew 23:37, Jesus laments, "Jerusalem, Jerusalem, who kills the prophets and stones those who have been sent to her! How often I wanted to gather your children together, the way a hen gathers her chicks under her wings, and you were unwilling."

Over and over, we see Jesus responding with compassion for people who are confused or in pain. The Bible is clear, God grieves when His children grieve. James 5:11

assures us, "The Lord is full of tenderness and mercy" (NLT).

But the way God feels is not the end of the story. God also *does* something in response to our pain.

Two Kinds of Pain

The Bible tells us a lot about what God does in response to our pain. And what He does depends on the type of pain we are experiencing.

To keep it simple, we'll divide pain into two categories:

- Pain we bring on ourselves—pain that results from our own personal choices.
- Pain from things we cannot control. In other words, pain that results from the evil choices of others, natural disasters, or other consequences of living in a broken world.

Let's start by looking at what God does in response to the pain we bring on ourselves.

Chapter 6

Perfume in the Gas Tank

WE ALL MAKE foolish choices. Sometimes we know better. Sometimes we don't. But the results are still the same. Unfortunately, our foolish choices are often followed by a good dose of pain.

So what is God's response to the pain we bring on ourselves?

The Lesson from Puff

A few years ago, I scrimped and saved and bought my dream car: a little silver convertible. I named it Puff—short for cream puff. (Yes, I know. Puff *is* a ridiculous name for a car!)

But oh, I love that car! And because I love Puff, I bring her in, on time, for every scheduled service. I make sure she is clean and waxed, and I park her at the far end of every parking lot—safe from dings from other car doors.

But what would you think if I said I was going to put perfume in Puff's gas tank? After all, wouldn't it be wonderful if Puff's engine smelled like a bouquet of flowers?

You'd think I was crazy. Right?

Well, obviously, you *would* be right! I *would* be crazy if I did that! How do we know putting perfume in Puff's gas tank would not be the smartest thing to do? We know because we've got a little black binder.

When I bought Puff, there was a black binder stashed in a slot inside the door. That binder holds a manufacturer's instruction manual filled with information about how to take care of my car.

It tells me what to put in the gas tank, how much air to put in the tires, and even when to take Puff in for checkups. It explains everything I need to know to keep Puff running smoothly.

When I saw that manual, do you think I tossed it out in a huff and announced, "No one's going to tell me what to do with my car!" Do you think I decided to ignore the manufacturer's advice and do whatever I thought was best?

Not a chance!

When I saw that manual, I opened it up and started reading. That's because I am convinced no one knows my car better than the manufacturer, and no one knows how to take care of it better than the folks who designed and created it.

I go through great pains and a lot of expense to follow my car's instruction manual—and I'll bet you do the same! We know if we follow the manufacturer's instructions, our cars will perform better, last longer, and we will enjoy them more.

Okay, so we know how to take care of our cars. But what does that have to do with our pain?

Another Bible Lesson

The Bible's Old Testament is filled with accounts of how the Israelites made foolish choices and landed in a world of hurt. Some of those choices were made in pure rebellion. Others were made in total ignorance. After all, human beings are incredibly complicated creatures.

It's not easy to know what is best for our lives. What's more, the Israelites did not have the benefit of a lot of things we have today—things like modern science and psychology. Yet even with those things and a whole lot more, we don't understand it all.

After years of research, scientists still can't figure out something as simple as what we should eat. Their advice on that subject changes like the weather. Plus, there are an awful lot of diseases we still don't know how to cure. We don't even completely understand our most basic physiological function—how our cells divide.

And that's just our physical bodies! We have mental, emotional, and spiritual parts, too. Plus, those parts are interconnected. What we do with one can affect the others—like negative thinking can make us physically sick.

We are complicated creatures. But that's not the end of it. Each of our lives touch other people's lives, and those relationships can be complicated, too. (Most of us have found this out the hard way!)

There are lots of things we don't understand about our lives and relationships. So how do we know what decisions to make? How do we know what to do? How do we know what will turn out best when all is said and done?

Introducing the Experts

In making decisions, some of us rely on counsel from parents, teachers, and friends. Some spend small fortunes on self-help books, classes, or even appointments with the experts.

That advice can be helpful, but different people can tell us different things. The advice one gives may be totally opposite from the advice we get from another. Even the experts don't have a perfect understanding about how our lives and relationships work best. (Just take a look at the poverty, disease, divorce rate, and conflict in the world around us.) So how in the world do we know whose advice to follow?

In making decisions, many folks simply ignore the experts, follow their own hearts, and do what they think is best. But it doesn't take long to learn things don't always end up the way we think they should. In fact, sometimes they end in disaster.

So where do we go for help? How do we judge the advice of others? Is there anyone who truly understands us? Is there anyone who can tell us what will always give us the best results in the end?

The Real Expert

You have probably already figured out the answer. There *is* someone who knows exactly how we work best: our Manufacturer—the One who designed and created us.

God knows every atom of our being. He knows exactly how He wired us—physically, mentally, emotionally, and spiritually. Plus, He knows how all our parts work together and how our relationships work best, too.

Because God understands everything about us and everyone around us, He knows what it takes for our lives to run smoothly. He knows what it takes for us to experience the deepest joy today and the greatest satisfaction tomorrow.

BACK TO GOD'S RESPONSE

God is the *real* expert about how we are designed to function. So what did He do when He saw people making ignorant decisions that caused them so much pain?

He picked a few people who loved Him, gave them a pen (or a couple of stone tablets), and downloaded His manufacturer's instruction manual.

Voilà! The Bible was born!

THE MANUAL

The Bible is filled with all kinds of wisdom about who God is and how we can live in a satisfying love relationship with Him—both now and for eternity. Yet it also includes all kinds of instructions about how our lives work best. In other words, the Bible is, in part, our manufacturer's instruction manual.

The information in the Bible addresses every aspect of our lives—from taking care of our physical bodies to our work, our relationships, our thought life, and of course our spiritual lives, too.

What's more, the Bible comes with an amazing promise. Joshua 1:8 says: "This book of the law shall not depart from your mouth, but you shall meditate on it day and night, so that you may be careful to do according to all that is written in it; for then you will make your way prosperous, and then you will achieve success."

Yep. The Bible promises, if we do what it says, we will be successful. That includes avoiding a whole lot of pain. Now that is quite a promise!

I have to admit, it took me years to trust that promise—especially when some of those instructions seemed a little strange to me. Sure, there were plenty that made a lot of sense—like Jesus' command to "Do to others as you would have them do to you" (Luke 6:31, NIV). And, of course, there's always, "You shall not murder" (Exodus 20:13, NIV).

But some of God's commands were a little harder to swallow—things like "Love your enemies" (Matthew 5:44), or "Give, and it will be given to you" (Luke 6:38). Others made me wonder if God just wanted to steal my fun or make me feel like a failure if I didn't live up to them.

But fast forward 48 years.

The Test of Time

One of the things I love about growing older is that you get a chance to witness the test of time. After decades of reading and studying the Bible and watching life unfold, I've seen the Bible's instructions play out in my life and the lives of others.

I've watched people who followed God's commands always end up with blessings, and those who ignored or disobeyed those commands end up with regrets—often huge regrets.

Oh, for a while it might look like the bad guys are winning or the good folks are ending up with the short end of the stick. But if you keep your eyes open and wait long enough, you will surely see the Bible prove true: "Do not be deceived, God is not mocked; for whatever a person sows, this he will also reap" (Galatians 6:7).

Not only does time prove the Bible to be true, but science continues to prove it as well. One easy-to-understand example is in the book of Deuteronomy. It's where God commands the Israelites to wash their hands after they touch a dead body.

Of course, today, that's no big news. We all know about germs and the danger of touching someone who died of a contagious disease. But keep in mind, Deuteronomy was written more than 3,000 years ago—long before anyone had ever heard of a germ or even a microscope, for that matter.

The ancient Israelites knew nothing about how diseases spread. But God knew, and He wanted to protect His children, so He simply told them to wash their hands.

He even told them how to wash them thoroughly. Those who obeyed that command—even though they didn't understand the science behind it—probably had no idea their obedience might be what kept them healthy and alive.

Another example is fasting. For thousands of years, the Bible has encouraged us to, periodically, fast from food. Forty-five years ago, when I began to research fasting, the only books I could find on the subject warned against it and claimed it could damage our health.

It puzzled me back then. I couldn't figure out why God would tell us to do something that would harm our bodies. As it turns out—He didn't.

Since then, scientists have learned that proper fasting can actually help our bodies heal. What's more, it can make us look younger. (Heaven knows, I'm all for that!)

Over and over, I've watched life play out and through the years I've learned the Bible bats a thousand. Its timeless wisdom always works. What's more, I've come to realize that much of the pain I've experienced in life was simply the result of not following its instructions.

As the years have gone by, it's become clearer and clearer that the Bible is, in fact, a *very* precious gift from a *very* loving Father—a Father who wants to keep His children far from needless pain.

A Final Word About the Bible

Before we move on, there's one more thing I'd like to say about the Bible. There are a lot of folks who don't like the Bible. They say it threatens their way of life. Yet, nothing could be farther from the truth.

Remember, God always gives us a choice. That's the beauty of it all. The Bible does not *make* us do anything. It simply tells us how we are designed to work best. We are free to do whatever we want. It just depends on how much pain we are willing to live with in the end.

Chapter 7

Don't Make Me

We've looked at one way God responded to the pain we bring on ourselves. When He saw us suffering from ignorant and rebellious choices, He gave us an instruction manual to help us make wise choices and avoid more needless pain.

Happy ending. Right?

Well, not so fast. You and I both know instructions don't work if we don't have the sense to follow them. We can be stubborn people. We're not always open to advice. What's more, Satan is still alive and kicking. He continues to feed us false promises and do his best to lead us astray.

All too often, we refuse to change course and end up bringing even more pain on ourselves. After all, what does God do when He sees we're running full steam toward disaster?

He responds like any loving parent.

Girls, Girls!

My mom and dad had six daughters in the span of a little more than seven years. They were wonderful parents but certainly had their hands full raising six little girls!

Kathy was the fearless one. She was three years old when mom walked into the kitchen and found her sitting on top of the refrigerator. We never figured out how Kathy got up there. But that was just the beginning of our struggle to keep her little feet on the ground.

I was not the daredevil Kathy was but I, too, had an unfortunate habit of learning things the hard way. I found out why you don't lick the metal railing at the bus stop in the middle of January. I also learned why it isn't a good idea to eat a whole bag of prunes in one sitting. (And those lessons were just the beginning …)

Margie was the oldest and spent most of her time trying to keep the rest us out of trouble. If she wasn't busy hiding everything small enough for Barbara to stick up her nose, she was trying to keep Janet from "de-furring" the cat, or prying Karen's head out from between the slats in the back of the kitchen chairs.

Yep, there was always something exciting going on at the Gordon house. With six rambunctious little girls, we certainly knew how to have our share of fun. Unfortunately for Mom and Dad, our definition of fun wasn't always teddy bears and tea parties.

We'd start out on some new adventure and then Mom or Dad would get that look on their face. Next we'd hear, "Stop that, girls! You're going to get hurt." Of course, by then we'd be having way too much fun to stop smack dab in the middle, so we'd keep going until we heard the dreaded words, "Don't make me …"

At that point, we had a choice: either wrap it up and go back to a life of boredom—or dig in our heels, have our fun, and face the music later. Of course, we could rest assured the "music" would include a little swat on our backsides reminding us to never do that again.

So why would Mom and Dad spank their sweet daughters? Obviously, it was because they wanted us to live to see another day.

They disciplined us because they loved us. And, wouldn't you know, God does the same thing when He sees His children are headed for trouble.

Another Choice

When God sees we're heading down the wrong path, He does what He can to warn us. If we ignore His warnings, He'll crank up a little pain to turn us around and get us back to safety.

Hebrews 12:5-6 tells us "My child, don't make light of the Lord's discipline, and don't give up when he corrects you. For the Lord disciplines those he loves" (NLT).

Like any loving Father, God wants His children to stay far away from danger. And He is willing to administer some pain to help us avoid a lot more pain later.

So how much pain does God use to discipline His children? Once again, the choice is ours.

If we change our ways when He warns us the first time, God doesn't need to turn the heat up too far. But if we dig in our heels and refuse to make changes, you can rest assured, He will do what it takes to get our attention.

A Faithful Father

In Hebrews 12:11, the Apostle Paul tells us, "No discipline is enjoyable while it is happening—it's painful! But afterward there will be a peaceful harvest of right living for those who are trained in this way" (NLT).

Even though God's discipline is painful, we can rest assured it will be good for us in the end. But even so, that doesn't necessarily mean we have to like it.

Well, you might be surprised to learn that God doesn't like it either. The Bible clearly tells us God does not like to hurt His children. Lamentations 3:31-33 says, "Though [the Lord] brings grief, he also shows compassion because of the greatness of his unfailing love. For he does not enjoy hurting people or causing them sorrow" (NLT).

In Jeremiah 26:2-3, God told Jeremiah to warn the Israelites about the dangerous things they were doing. God let Jeremiah know He wanted them to stop so He would not have to discipline them and cause them pain.

Sure enough, God loves us, and He takes no delight in disciplining us. But, again, we are the ones who choose the pain.

If we go astray, we force God to do what it takes to bring us back to safety.

And out of His great love for us, He will.

One More Thing

Before we move on, I'd like to cover one more thing.

Some of us have ignored God's discipline and lived to regret it. After all, we all make mistakes and foolish choices, and each comes with its own set of consequences. Like the Bible says—we reap what we sow.

Sometimes our consequences are relatively small—sort of like a blip on the screen. Other times they are gargantuan—like an atom bomb that leaves our life, and sometimes the lives of our loved ones, in ashes.

So what do we do if we've blown it—and I mean, really blown it?

Whether we end up with a blip or a bomb, the Bible tells us what we can do.

- First, sincerely ask God and the people we hurt to forgive us. Then pray God will bless and heal those we hurt and give them the strength to forgive.
- Next comes the big one. (This one feels like we're jumping off a cliff but will end up being one of the best decisions we've ever made.) Totally surrender our life to God and ask Him to do *whatever* it takes to help us change our ways.
- Last but not least, thank God that He is the great redeemer. He is not only able, but He is more than willing to make something beautiful out of the messes we have made.

Rest assured, if we swallow our pride and tackle each step with a sincere heart, God will turn the leftovers of our lives into a beautiful buffet.

By the way, we can never be so bad or fall so far that God cannot catch us. God is merciful, and He can do anything. In Isaiah 43:19, He says, "Behold, I am going to do something new, now it will spring up; will you not be aware of it? I will even make a roadway in the wilderness, rivers in the desert."

So if you feel like you've absolutely blown it, and you're lost in the wilderness or dying in a desert, don't give up or despair. Put your life in His hands—every bit of it. Then stand back and watch our amazing God do what only He can do—make beauty out of the ashes of our lives.

Chapter 8

Another Kind of Pain

It wasn't hard for me to understand why God allows us to experience the pain we bring on ourselves. (After all, we *do* bring it on ourselves.) But there was another kind of pain I struggled to understand.

Why would a loving God allow us to experience pain we had no part in causing? Plagues, accidents, natural disasters happen. Other people hurt us, too. Why does God allow us to experience pain from things over which we have no control? For me that was, by far, the hardest question.

Yet, over time, an answer began to take shape. It all began one morning when I knocked on my sister's front door.

Another Kind of Pain

Karen's Kitchen

My sister Karen opened the door with a broom and dustpan in her hand. She greeted me and then led me to her kitchen and told me a story I will never forget.

Only a few minutes earlier she and her four daughters had been making breakfast in their tiny kitchen. While they were cooking someone accidentally left an empty dish on a hot burner. They were working away when, suddenly ... BANG! The dish exploded and shards of glass shot through the air.

I looked down and saw the burn marks scattered over the linoleum floor. On top of each was a hardened drop of what had once been red-hot, molten glass. Then I noticed shards of glass imbedded in the kitchen walls. Those razor-sharp projectiles had shot through the air with such force that they planted themselves deep into the drywall.

Karen told me she and her four daughters were only a few feet away from the dish when it exploded. I stood, horrified, thinking about what could have happened. Yet there was my sister, standing next to me, apparently uninjured.

When I looked down at her dustpan filled with glass shards, I haltingly asked, "Is everyone okay?" Karen shook her head and told me everyone was fine. The only injury was a tiny scratch on the back of Stephanie's, her oldest daughter's, hand.

I was flooded with relief but could hardly believe it. You see, Karen has a small galley kitchen—a row of cabinets on opposite walls with a narrow walkway in between. There was nowhere to hide from an exploding dish only a few feet away. I stood in awe trying to figure out how my precious family could have escaped virtually uninjured.

Suddenly, my nieces came bounding through the door. Each gave me a hug and began to tell me about their adventure that morning.

There it was—a kitchen that looked like the crime scene in a slasher movie. And there they were—my nieces and sister—standing healthy and whole in front of me. I had no doubt God, in His mercy, had blessed us all with a miracle.

I thanked Him and then bent down to pick up two shards of glass at my feet. Until this day, I keep them in my desk drawer as a constant reminder that the only things that can touch my life are the things God allows.

Boundaries

What a lesson God taught that morning! And as I read my Bible in the following months, God continued to drive that lesson home.

In the first chapter of the book of Job, Satan shows up in God's throne room. During their little get-together,

Another Kind of Pain

God gives Satan permission to test Job—but only within certain boundaries. God told Satan he could do whatever he wanted with Job's possessions, but He would not allow Satan to harm Job physically.

There it was in black and white. God told Satan what he could and could not do.

I ran across another example of Satan needing God's permission when Jesus told Simon Peter, "Simon, Simon, behold, Satan has demanded permission to sift you like wheat; but I have prayed for you, that your faith may not fail; and you, when once you have turned again, strengthen your brothers" (Luke 22:31-32).

I breathed a sigh of relief when I learned Satan cannot test us without God's permission. What's more, Isaiah 42:3 gives us even better news. It says, "A bruised reed [God] will not break and a dimly burning wick He will not extinguish." The Apostle Paul puts it this way: "We are afflicted in every way, but not crushed; perplexed, but not despairing; persecuted, but not forsaken; struck down, but not destroyed" (2 Corinthians 4:8-9). He even tells us, "God is faithful, so He will not allow you to be tempted beyond what you are able" (1 Corinthians 10:13).

Beyond a doubt, Scripture is clear. God puts limits on what Satan can do to us. And, as I learned in Karen's kitchen, God can stop any pain He chooses.

Another Question

So that was how the lesson began. God gave me comfort in knowing everything that touches us has been sifted through His loving hands. What's more, He will not allow us to experience more pain or temptation than He will give us the strength to handle.

Although I found a lot of comfort in those truths, something still troubled me—another looming question: "If God can stop any pain He chooses, why doesn't He choose to stop it all?"

Chapter 9

The Plan

As I look back, I marvel at how God patiently crafted the answers to my questions. Lesson after lesson, layer upon layer—He revealed each truth, then blended them together until a satisfying answer finally emerged. What's more, He used all kinds of things—little birds, glass dishes, passages of Scripture.

In the same way, He crafted His answer about why He won't stop all our pain. This time He started with a trainer named George.

Meet George

I crawled out of bed before the crack of dawn, brushed my teeth, and jumped into my clothes. Minutes later, I pulled into the parking lot just before the gym doors opened.

George was the gym's best trainer. I'd watched him from afar for a very long time. He got results—great results—month after month, client after client. He even trained professional athletes—household names—people *even I* had heard of.

Yep. George was the best, and everybody knew it.

George and I would always say hello, and every now and then we would chat. I was on a pretty tight budget at the time—even the monthly gym fees were a stretch—so I knew hiring George to train me was completely out of the question.

Then one day, out of the blue, George offered to give me a free training session! All I had to do was show up at 5:00 a.m. the next morning.

I was elated! Free advice from the best trainer I knew! I counted the minutes until 5:00—ready for an hour of torture.

And George did not disappoint.

George cleaned my clock. He pushed me harder than I had ever been pushed. He paid no attention to my gasps for air, winces, and even a groan or two. George knew what it would take to get results—and he was going to make sure I got them.

I did my very best to follow George's instructions. I pushed. I pulled. I ran. I jumped. I did it all without question, until finally—yes, *finally*—he told me to stop.

When I said goodbye to George that morning, I could barely walk. I was totally exhausted and dripping

THE PLAN

with sweat—a hurtin' puppy for sure. But as I hobbled through the parking lot and crawled into my car, I found myself smiling ear to ear.

That smile grew out of an absolute certainty that everything I'd gone through that morning would be worth it. If I kept it up and did what George taught me, I would surely be a very happy camper in the end.

THE ULTIMATE TRAINER

That was quite a morning—one I'll never forget—but not because of a killer workout. The part I'll always remember is what happened when I got home.

After I took a shower and got ready for the day, I opened my Bible and began to read, "He trains my hands for battle; my arms can bend a bow of bronze ... your right hand sustains me; your help has made me great" (Psalm 18:34-35, NIV).

As I read that passage, the words sounded eerily familiar. I thought about my aching arms and the challenges I'd faced that morning. I'd tackled each with all the eagerness anyone could possibly muster before the crack of dawn. I trusted George and his training plan for me. I knew the cold hard truth. There is a price to pay for strength and endurance. And that morning I got a brutal reminder that the price can include a good bit of pain.

I looked down, again, at Psalm 18. "He trains my hands for battle … your help has made me great." I thought for a moment—then smiled.

Well, what do you know! George was not the only one with a training plan for me. That verse was a beautiful reminder that God has a training plan, too. What's more, God's plan includes a magnificent goal for every one of His children. "For those whom he foreknew he also predestined to become conformed to the image of his Son" (Romans 8:29, ESV).

God's goal for us is to be like Jesus. But how in the world can we reach that goal? After all, that's a pretty high calling, and we've got a few things working against us. We face a formidable foe who relentlessly tries to destroy us. And every day we are caught in an epic battle between good and evil.

Enter a God who longs to see His children win that battle. He wants to help us develop the strength and endurance to triumph in all that is good. But just as there is a price to pay for physical strength and endurance, strength of character and an enduring spirit do not come easily or without pain.

The good news is our loving Father is a seasoned and flawless trainer. The pain He allows will not destroy us. Instead, according to Psalm 18, that pain will "make us great."

The Plan

Just as George puts a weight in our hands to help us build a muscle, God puts challenges in our lives to help us build a much greater treasure. George is training our bodies, but God is training our hearts and souls.

God puts difficult people in our lives to help us learn how to love. His roadblocks help us learn patience. The failures He allows make us humble and kind. Even the horrible losses and tragedies teach us perseverance and perspective.

Our God has a training plan, and it can be painful. But the Bible assures us it will be worth it. "Consider it all joy, my brethren, when you encounter various trials, knowing that the testing of your faith produces endurance. And let endurance have its perfect result, so that you may be perfect and complete, lacking in nothing" (James 1:2-4).

And so God continues His quest to help His children become like Jesus—perfect and complete, lacking in nothing. He brilliantly uses the pain of this world to fill us with wisdom and compassion—to soften our hearts, strengthen our character, and to build the endurance and integrity we need to love well and live lives that matter in the end.

SOMETHING BEAUTIFUL

So why doesn't God stop all our pain? Of course, we won't know all His reasons until we stand before Him. But we know one reason beyond a doubt—it's because He loves you and me.

He wants us to experience the delight and adventure of a goal greater than we can imagine. He wants us to know the love and companionship of Him as our trainer and guide. He wants to help us be like Jesus—perfect and complete, lacking in nothing. And then He wants us to share the hope and healing we have found in Him so that others, too, might know the joy and comfort of His glorious love.

Once again, God turns the pain of this broken world into something beautiful. And, once again, another piece of the puzzle falls into place.

Chapter 10

Beyond Pain

I LOOKED BACK TO the fateful day when I asked our parish priest the Big One: "Why would a good God …?" I had hoped for a simple, satisfying answer. Instead, I got a springboard into a decades-long search for truth.

As years passed, God provided answers to my steady stream of questions. I found comfort in learning our heavenly Father chose paradise—not pain—for His children. Instead, Satan tempted, and mankind chose to introduce the pain.

But God refused to give us over to Satan's plan for our destruction. Instead, He brilliantly leveraged the pain to make us more like Jesus.

And so, the answers God mercifully gave to that point were enough for me. I lived for years in peace. That is, until a season of pain and sorrow stretched beyond my understanding.

The Season

Before I go further, I want to assure you I am very aware the pain I have experienced may be nothing compared to the pain you have been through. I don't know the tragedies of your past or the torments you face today. All I know is that horrific and unthinkable things can happen to innocent people.

Yet even though God has spared me from many of life's tragedies, I too, have gone through seasons when the anguish of life seemed more than I could bear.

It was one of those seasons for me—a steady stream of disappointments and losses: a failed business, an empty bank account, an accident, a painful injury, a shattered romance, a hopeless future—too many funerals of people I loved.

Years passed. Each time I struggled to my feet, something else came crashing down around me. How many more times could I find the strength to crawl out of the rubble and start over again?

The Prayer

It had been a brutal day. I lay in bed clinging to a fading hope in a God who had been silent for so long. Memories of many prayers prayed in desperation—prayers prayed with every bit of strength I had. Yet here I was, years later, with no end to the pain in sight.

I closed my eyes, stifled a sob, and prayed the only prayer I had left. It was an honest prayer—no use in pretending. After all, He knew my heart. I might as well tell Him outright.

"God, I am so weary. I trusted You and Your plan for me. I've worked so hard and searched for Your guidance, but time after time, things end in disaster. Everything just falls apart.

"Lord, I'm tired of failure. Tired of pain. Tired of goodbyes to people I love. Why won't You do something to change things? Why won't You have mercy on me?"

Out of nowhere, a verse came to mind, "Behold, I have refined you, but not as silver; I have tested you in the furnace of affliction" (Isaiah 48:10).

Yes, a timely reminder. But not one I wanted to hear.

"Lord, I know You want to refine me. You want me to be like Jesus. But if this is what it takes, I don't want to be like Jesus. The price is too high. I can't take it.

I opened my eyes and stared at the ceiling.

Was He listening? Did He hear me? Did He even care? Had I been fooling myself all this time thinking He would answer my prayers?

But who else could I turn to? No one else had the power to change the things beyond my control. I had to admit—it was Him or nothing.

So I continued, "Lord, You are my only hope. I have no one else to turn to. I'll try my best to keep moving forward until You call me home. But I barely have the strength to put one foot in front of the other. You're going to have to help me, Lord."

With that, I sat up, turned on the light, and reached for the Bible on my nightstand. Maybe I'd find some comfort there.

A Familiar Passage

My Bible fell open to Hebrews chapter 11. A familiar passage that some call the "Faith Hall of Fame."

The first 34 verses lifted my spirit. They told of God's faithfulness to those who trusted Him. They told of Noah who obeyed God by building a massive ark. In turn, he, his family, and a host of animals all survived the great flood.

Then there was Abraham. He chose to follow God even though he did not know where God was leading. In turn, God blessed him for his faithfulness and made him the father of many nations.

Moses also made it into the Faith Hall of Fame. He obeyed God against all odds and led the Israelites out of Egypt. When they reached the Red Sea, the Egyptian army was hot on their trail and closing in fast. God miraculously saved them by parting the waters and letting the

Israelites cross. When they were safe on the other side, God closed the waters and drowned the entire Egyptian army.

The passage went on to tell of other men and women God blessed, in miraculous ways, because of their trust and obedience.

Yes, God can do miracles. Maybe there was hope for me.

But my heart began to sink as verses 35-38 took a darker turn. Those verses told of men and women of faith whose stories did not have such happy endings.

Those verses said "others were tortured, ... others experienced mockings and scourgings, yes, also chains and imprisonment. They were stoned, *they were sawn in two*, they were tempted, they were put to death with the sword; they went about in sheepskins, in goatskins, being destitute, afflicted, ill-treated *(men of whom the world was not worthy)*, wandering in deserts and mountains and caves and holes in the ground" (emphasis added).

That was not the first time I had read that passage. But on that night, the horror of those verses touched a deeper place in my heart than it had touched before.

I was confused. I was upset. Why would God refuse to help them in the midst of their torture and pain? "God, is this how You treat Your faithful children?" I could not reconcile the concept of a loving God with that kind of suffering—a suffering that continues to this day.

I thought about the tens of thousands of Sudanese believers hacked to death by swords of their fellow countrymen for one reason—only one reason. They loved Jesus.

Men in orange jumpsuits kneeling on the sand—waiting to be beheaded by the masked ISIS cowards standing behind them. All for one reason—only one reason. They would not renounce their faith in Jesus.

Hundreds of people in villages in India slaughtered, burned, raped, beaten. Fathers in China and North Korea, taken from their families—imprisoned in dark, filthy, hellholes—tortured for years—again, for one reason—only one reason. They would not deny Jesus as their Lord.

Is that what God has for His faithful and pure?

And what about all the innocent children abducted and abused? Spouses beaten. Loved ones murdered. Every day, all over the world, people do brutal things to innocent people.

It sickened me.

Why does God allow it? Doesn't He see it? Doesn't He care?

Yes. I had to admit. God sees every bit of it. But what does He do?

As I began to weep, God gently reminded me of exactly what He does.

He weeps, too.

Yes, God reminded me that He understands our struggles. He knows our pain—and then some. He was tortured—nailed to a cross—suspended only by the spikes that pierced His wrists and feet. I could rest assured that He understands our pain. He suffered for us so one day we might know the hope of heaven and freedom from this broken world.

Yes, God weeps. But at that moment, a verse—a promise—came to mind. "God causes *all* things to work together for good to those who love God, to those who are called according to His purpose" (Romans 8:28, emphasis added).

God reminded me that He can make something good out of everything that happens to His children. Even the horrors of persecution, torture, and unspeakable pain.

But how? How could He make something good out of all those atrocities?

That is what He showed me next.

Chapter 11

The Million

GOD CAN DO anything. I'd heard it all my life. He can even bring good out of evil.

I'd read about it in the Bible. I'd heard about it in the testimonies of people God saved from horrible things. I'd watched it happen in the lives of my friends. I'd even experienced it in my own life. God can take a hopeless situation and turn it into a celebration—light from darkness, beauty from ashes, joy from despair.

Yes, He could do it. Of that I was sure—at least I was sure He could do it in most cases. But Romans 8:28 tells us He can do it in *every* case for those of us who love Him. The verse is clear: "God causes *all* things to work together for good to those who love God, to those who are called according to His purpose" (Romans 8:28, emphasis added).

Yet as I thought about the evil and cruelty in this world, the idea that everything could work for good seemed more than I could fathom. How was it possible that God could make something good out of all the dreadful things people do and all the accidents and disasters that happen?

The answer to that question began to unfold at the end of another busy day.

THE UNFOLDING

It was a cold winter evening, and I was ready for a good night's sleep. Before I lay down, I opened my Bible to 2 Chronicles—the story of Hezekiah. He was a king in ancient Judah who loved God and served Him faithfully.

When Hezekiah became king, he destroyed the Israelites' idols, repaired the temple of the Lord, and turned the hearts of the people back to God. In turn, God blessed Hezekiah and all of Israel.

The passage continues with other stories of Hezekiah's faithfulness. I was closing in on the end of the chapter when a verse stopped me in my tracks: "God left [Hezekiah] alone only to test him, that He might know all that was in his heart" (2 Chronicles 32:31).

Hmmm. What was that about?

Why would God test Hezekiah? It didn't make sense to me. Hezekiah loved God and was doing great things. Why wouldn't God just continue to bless him? What's more, didn't God already know what was in his heart and what he would do? After all, God is God. He knows everything.

I closed my Bible, turned out the light, and laid in bed with my eyes wide open. For some reason, I could not shake those questions.

As minutes crawled by, I continued to ponder why God would test such a godly man. Why would He put someone to the test who was cranking so hard to do right?

The longer I lay there, the clearer it became that I wasn't going to get to sleep any time soon. I might as well do a little research. So I padded across the hall to my office, grabbed a few books, sat down, and began to read.

Sure enough, I found plenty of passages that described how God tested His people. When God told Moses about His plan to give the Israelites manna, God said, "*I will test them in this* to see whether or not they will follow my instructions" (Exodus 16:4, NLT, emphasis added).

The book of Judges tells us about a time when the Israelites turned away from God. It also tells us how God responded. God said He would no longer remove other nations from the Promised Land. He let those nations remain *to test Israel*—to see whether or not they would follow His ways.

Of course, the entire book of Job tells what happened when God gave Satan permission to test Job, a "blameless and upright" man.

The more examples I found, the more confused I got. It was clear God tests all kinds of people. Even the good ones. But why?

It was late, my eyelids were heavy, and morning would be there all too soon. I sighed, returned my books to the shelf, and came to my only conclusion.

I'd think about that tomorrow.

THE REVELATION

It was the end of another busy day. My Bible lay across my lap as I struggled to keep my eyes open. I wanted to read at least a few verses. I was not expecting to find anything earth-shattering or answers to any particular questions. I just wanted to end the day with God's thoughts fresh in my mind.

I turned to 1 Peter, chapter one. At first nothing was sinking in—just black words on a page. But as I continued my focus sharpened, and the message came into view.

I read about the living hope of Jesus' resurrection. Then I read about the imperishable inheritance reserved in heaven for those who love God.

This was getting interesting.

I went on to the next two verses: "In this you greatly rejoice, even though now for a little while, if necessary, you have been distressed by various trials, *so that the proof of your faith*, being more precious than gold which is perishable, even though tested by fire, *may be found to result in praise and glory and honor at the revelation of Jesus Christ*" (1 Peter 1:6-7, emphasis added).

I paused for a moment. My heart stirred.

Did that say what I think it said?

I read it again.

I think so.

I read it again. This time, slowly.

Was it really that simple?

The Answer

I could hardly believe it. After decades of searching—there it was. And it really was that simple.

I had read that passage dozens of times, and every other time I had missed it. Yet there it was in black and white—what appeared to be the answer to my question.

Those verses seemed to be telling me God tests us with trials so we can prove our faith in Him. He does not do it because He wants to see us suffer. He does it out of love for us—so the proof of our faith will earn for us praise, glory, and honor when He returns.

I sat for a moment and pondered that passage. It had never occurred to me that God might allow us to experience pain so we could earn rewards in heaven.

I began to mull that over.

The Bible clearly teaches that our good works can never get us into heaven. Only faith in Jesus can do that. It tells us "For by grace you have been saved through faith; and that not of yourselves, it is the gift of God; *not as a result of works, so that no one may boast*" (Ephesians 2:8-9, emphasis added).

Yet the Bible also teaches that, once we get to heaven, God will reward us for the good things we have done. "For we must all appear before the judgment seat of Christ, so that each of us may receive what is due us for the things done while in the body, whether good or bad" (2 Corinthians 5:10, NIV).

I looked again at 1 Peter 1:6-7, "… you have been distressed by various trials, so that the proof of your faith … may be found to result in praise and glory and honor …"

Yep, sure enough. That verse was clear. God allows trials so we can prove our faith in Him and, in turn, receive praise, glory, and honor.

But praise, glory, and honor? I wondered what that looked like.

Suddenly I remembered a verse that gives us a clue, "Things which eye has not seen and ear has not heard, and which have not entered the heart of man, all that God has prepared for those who love Him" (1 Corinthians 2:9).

Simply put, God's rewards are beyond our imagination.

I stopped. I thought for a moment. Then I sat upright as my mind began to race.

So although it was mankind who chose pain, God gives us a chance to turn that pain into indescribable blessings. What's more, our pain will end one day but the rewards He gives us will last forever.

A finite investment for an infinite return—a wise investment, indeed!

That was it! I finally saw it.

Our loving Father did it again. He turned our pain into something beautiful. What's more, He really *does* cause all things to work together for good for those who love Him.

The Peace

One by one, the pieces fell in place and the lesson continued to take shape.

Again I realized that what I was learning was not the only answer to my question. I had no doubt the theology books were filled with explanations I might never know.

What's more, there were probably many more answers no one but God could understand.

But God knew I didn't need more answers. That night He gave me exactly what I needed to find the peace for which I'd been searching—peace in knowing He loves us, and He is gloriously good.

THE BATTLE

Because God is good, He uses our pain to test us—to give us a battle, if you will. For if we never have a battle, we'll never have a victory. If we never have a victory, we'll never have a reward. And God's rewards are more than worth all the endurance and strength it takes to win them.

Sometimes God gives us rewards here on earth. Sometimes He asks us to wait until heaven. Either way, we can rest assured His rewards are beyond our wildest hopes and dreams.

But God's mercy and kindness do not stop there. He does not let His children flounder. Instead, He helps us win our battles. He begins by giving us strength.

The Bible tells us He gives us the strength to conquer every challenge we face. The Apostle Paul tells us, in no uncertain terms, "I can do all things through Him who strengthens me" (Philippians 4:13).

God even goes a step further. He stays by our side as we fight. He assures us, "I will never leave you nor forsake you" (Joshua 1:5, NIV). In fact, He even cheers us on. He reminds us, "Be strong and do not lose courage, for there is reward for your work" (2 Chronicles 15:7).

What an amazing God we serve and what a gift of love He gives us—a chance to turn our temporary pain into rewards that we can enjoy forever. All He asks of us is to remain faithful to Him through it all.

The Choice

And so, once again, our heavenly Father reveals His limitless love for His children. He longs to bless us, and because He loves us He always gives us a choice.

Each time He gives us a battle and we face disappointment and pain, we can choose to be bitter and angry, or we can choose to be faithful to Him. Although our bitterness and anger might bring us fleeting satisfaction, it will only bring more bitterness and anger in the end.

But our God has a better plan. That's why He asks us to trust Him. For He is like a wealthy father who gives His children a choice—we can have an ice cream cone now or a million dollars later. Then He stands back and quietly whispers, over and over, "Take the million."

I pray that, in the midst of your battle, you'll hear His gentle whisper and train your eyes on what you cannot see. I pray you'll lean on Him for strength and rest in knowing His love for you is strong. What's more, His plans for you are good, and He will not allow you to be tested beyond what you are able.

Those are His promises, and He is the promise keeper—a good God and a faithful, loving Father. So trust Him, train your eyes on Him, and, above all, take the million.

*Therefore, those also who suffer
according to the will of God shall entrust their souls
to a faithful Creator in doing what is right.*
1 Peter 4:19

Thank You ...

As I write the final words of this manuscript, I look back with immense gratitude for the precious friends and family who have encouraged, supported, and prayed for me along the way. You have blessed and inspired me in so many ways. I could never have written this book without you.

A special thanks to my gifted reviewers who prayed for me then took time to read, reflect, and provide such insightful comments and suggestions. You saw what I could not see. You gently challenged what needed to be challenged. Above all, you encouraged me more than you will ever know. My sincerest thanks to Donna Beverly, Carolyn Davis, Margie Davis, Tara McCown, Donna Moody, Meg Patterson, Martha Schuon, Dan Simmons, Ellen Stepat, Tomme Stevenson, Dean O. Webb, Becky Williams, Catherine Williams, and Cindy Williams. Thank you for your priceless friendship and the invaluable contributions you have made to this manuscript.

Thank You ...

An immense thank you to Jodi Carlson, my dear friend and editor. You have always been there when I needed you. I cherish your eagle eye and your wonderful encouragement that always seems to come when I need it most. Thank you for all you do and the gracious, loving way you do it.

To my dear friend Dori Dacre. I cannot thank you enough for helping me finish the cover. You are an extraordinary talent, a wonderful encourager, a kindred spirit, and a beautiful friend.

Many thanks to my lifelong friends and prayer partners, Sandy Schoepke and Martha Schuon. I have no doubt that the countless hours we have spent before the throne are reflected in every word of this book. Your prayers, love, support, and friendship are gifts I will always cherish.

And finally, my deepest appreciation to my precious family. Your faithful love, kindness, and encouragement have carried me across every finish line. It is my honor to call you family as we share the joys and sorrows of life. You will always be my greatest earthly treasure.

If you would like to contact Patti
or read other books she has written,
visit www.PattiGordon.com.

Patti loves to hear from her readers.

CPSIA information can be obtained
at www.ICGtesting.com
Printed in the USA
FSHW020128040122
87317FS